Wit and
Wisdom
from the
Piano Bench

**50 Witty and 50 Wise
Ways to Inspire Aspiring Musicians**

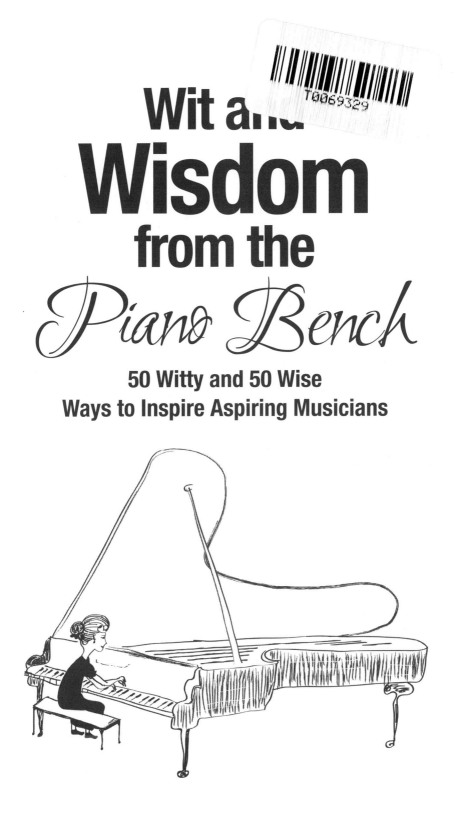

Production: Dovetree Productions, Inc.
Production Coordinator: Betsy Henrichs
Printing: Vicks, Yorkville NY USA
ISBN: 978-1-61677-709-8

Dedication

This book is dedicated to
Alexa Suzanne Guy
and
James Schambeau Guy,
my extra-musical grandchildren

The author is indebted to
Tonya M. Holland
and
Abbie Rae Menard
for their
editorial and
creative contributions

Tonya's Take

Years ago, as I sat in a workshop for the Tidewater Music Teachers Forum (TMTF) in Virginia Beach, Virginia. I was mesmerized by Suzanne Guy. I remember telling myself in that moment that I had to attain the qualifications I needed to do what she was doing... inspiring all of us to be better teachers. After I became more active in TMTF and the Music Teachers National Association (MTNA), I observed Suzanne's many accomplishments: editing, writing music books and articles, and leading panels at national conventions. I realized that I needed more instruction.

I wanted to go back to school to work on my DMA, but in order to pass the audition, I needed to refine my playing. Suzanne Guy, my role model, accepted me as an adult student and I was thrilled! Every lesson contained gems like those in this book. She had a way of explaining things as if in parables so I could relate and understand easily in order to revive the color in my music and empower my technique.

As I was finishing school, I kept in touch with Suzanne. One day as we were talking, a light bulb went off over my head. "Someone needs to write a book about you," I said. "And I'm just the person to do it." Luckily, she agreed! Suzanne is a confident but modest soul, and I was certain the piano world needed to know more of her teaching techniques and wisdom.

There are enough materials from her years of teaching to provide encyclopedic volumes of guidance. This book of *Wit and Wisdom* is a small taste of what is to come. It has been a privilege to spend time with such a gracious and brilliant woman, pianist, and teacher. I consider myself a facilitator of her voice, since Parkinson's Disease has diminished her ability to type. It has not, however, diminished her ability to edit, create, and continue to inspire music teachers around the world.

~ Tonya M. Holland, Harrisonburg, VA

Foreword

IF you know Suzanne Guy and have heard her presentations, you have been impressed with the creativity, wit, and deep knowledge of the piano teaching field she possesses. Hers is a rare combination of insight into a student's world, and an uncanny ability to elicit profound musical expression from each student.

IF you are reading this book without knowing her personally, hold on tight for a refreshing excursion of humor and insight into the world of piano study. Tens of thousands claim piano teaching as their profession. Few have matched the success of Suzanne Guy, whose students have achieved the highest marks in regional and national competitions and whose impact on the lives of her students, their parents, her colleagues and acquaintances remains indelible throughout a lifetime.

~ Marvin Blickenstaff
Internationally Renowned Piano Pedagogue

OVERTURE:
The Piano's Perspective

For more years than I can remember, I've been the focal point of a large square room – twenty by twenty to be exact. This very moment I'm sitting slightly off center waiting for the first student's greeting, and anticipating delight in the weekday visits of dozens of piano students. I cannot bear to think how lonely it would be if I had no visitors.

There are days I wouldn't trade my place with anyone or anything. Long before the birds begin to sing, someone is warming up, so I start my calisthenics early. I am sure the ritual of daily exercise is one of the reasons I am blessed with long life. In the middle of the day I get a break and return to a dormant state before a rush of activity every afternoon. For students whose schedules are full, I am often their last stop. Even so, I am grateful that they somehow fit me in.

Sometimes I feel as if I hold the keys to the kingdom, the kingdom of piano literature. How did I get so lucky? I have been privileged to produce Beethoven sonatas, Liszt and Chopin etudes, Bach inventions, preludes and fugues, Mozart concerti and more. What is better than one piano? Two pianos. I never will forget the day when a twin piano moved in right beside me. Now the two of us can host ensembles for up to four or even six pianists.

My inner workings are not visible, but therein lies my special power. Unless you take me apart and expose the complex network of levers inside, you would never guess the source of my power. My hammers take a journey of several inches en route to their bounce against the strings. My deep resonant tone is one of life's great mysteries, considering it's a scant 3/8's of an inch from top to bottom of each key.

Before someone touches one of my keys, I wait and wonder what kind of attack is coming. I've endured those who punch, hit, poke and beat up on me and savored others who press, caress, stroke and "love me tender." My best feature is my ability to mimic the sounds of nature (thunder, drizzle, rainbows, wind), as well as birds, animals, and every other instrument – including the voice. On a good day, students share with me their heartfelt secrets and even shed a few tears from time to time. There is a connection between my keys and the pianists' fingertips that shall remain a mystery. The result is pure magic.

How To Use This Book

There are several options:

If you want a quick overview, read straight through.

If you want a chuckle for the day, start with the first 25 pages of *Wit* marked with a wink in the contents.

If you want more substance, read the next 27 pages of *Wisdom* marked with a brainstorm.

If you need a specific tip, check the table of contents, or pair a few together of your choice. For example, Wit #14, 15, and 47, could match with Wisdom #5!

Contents

Your Daily Chuckle

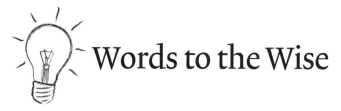

Words to the Wise

Wit

❶ Für Elise Overload

A sign seen in a piano store ...

"Please Limit Your Attempts at Für Elise to ONE!"

❷ Brain Strain

The see-through container of a simulated human brain caught the eye of a new student.

Curious, she asked:

"Is that a real brain?"

"Yes. I borrowed it from a student since he wasn't using it."

Dark Side ❸

After an unprepared student sat through several lessons in a row with no apparent progress, I said

"Uh-oh,

I may have to show my dark side."

Piano Pizzazz ❹

Piano playing is often too plain.

Perfect your own

❺ Headlines We May Never See

BREAKING NEWS!

"8-Year Old Discovers Bach!"

"Soccer Player Skips Practice to Memorize a Sonatina."

"Siblings Fight Over Who Gets the Most Practice Time."

"Parents Offer to Pay for All the Overtime the Teacher has Given Their Child."

Rubato ❻

Rubato

...is the amateur's last hope!
~ Ruth Harte

Chopin explained rubato in words first: "A free walk on firm ground. The accompaniment, usually in the left hand, must be predictably steady while the melody breathes as if sung, projecting subtlety and nuance."

The romantic composer further illustrated rubato with a lighted candle. He asked his student to blow gently and watch the flame flicker and then return to its vertical position. Such freedom must always be controlled.

Nobody's Perfect ❼

Repeating a mistake is a bigger mistake.

Musicians might well learn a couple of lessons from the Itsy Bitsy spider – repetition and resilience. "Out came the sun and dried up all the rain, so the Itsy Bitsy spider climbed up the spout again."

❽ Thomas Edison's Formula

Thomas Edison never failed – he just found 10,000 ways that did not work.

A good teacher will hear a student play a piece and find 25 things wrong. It's a dilemma – like a mosquito that visits a nudist colony – where do you strike first?

An inexperienced teacher might unwittingly address the litany of problems, overwhelming the student. Instead, pick your battles and save a student.

❾ Vladimir and Van ~ Known for Tone

Vladimir Horowitz had the uncanny ability to project his sound by placing his ears in the 20th row.

One of Van Cliburn's favorite memories of his mother (who was also his first and only teacher until he studied at Juilliard) was her instruction to listen for the "eye" of the sound.

Beginnings and Endings

When new students transfer to my studio, they must bring to their first lesson a short essay answering the question **"Why do you want to continue piano lessons?"** This one I saved because it is such an original description...

"The subject of music is so interesting to me because it is like a squishy lump of clay. You can mold it, shape it, and bend it anyway you want to...with any instrument in the world from a tissue box guitar to a big old bassoon."
~ Boy, age 12

Most people have plenty of initiative.

What they lack is...

FINISHitive!

⓫ It Starts with a Dream

Do you dream of becoming an
excellent pianist?

That's not enough.
You must wake up
and get busy!

Everyone Has Time ⓬

Do less, but focus more.

If you have one minute to accomplish a goal at the piano, make every second count. It's challenging to find big chunks of time. Many have known the value of coming to the point quickly, with this popular phrase:

"I would have written a shorter letter, but I didn't have the time."

~ Many sources claim authorship for this quote

Pedal Power ⓭

The next time you depress the damper pedal, think of it as a unique resource and proceed with caution. In fact, the pedal is like a knife. It can be a useful tool for slicing bread or carving meat, or a deadly weapon in the wrong hands.

"Less is more" applies as you listen carefully to the resonance the damper pedal offers.

⑭ Serenading is Not Practicing

Many musicians suffer from

"wishful hearing."

We all have a tendency to serenade ourselves at the piano. Listen as objectively as possible.

⑮ Play It Again, Sam

You played that so well!

Better try it again to make sure it wasn't an accident.

Dress Code 16

If your accompaniment is making more of an impression than your melody, it's exactly like putting on a stunning outfit and letting your underwear show.

Mozart Sonata in C, K.545

Melody

Accompaniment

The notes above are all present.
But only the melody is prominent

Planning Ahead 17

Plan ahead.

Like a chess player, you must strategize your practice session, making sure you can start from anywhere. Chess players plan 12 moves ahead.

⑱ Breakthrough

Think of a **breakthrough**,
not a b-r-e-a-k-d-o-w-n.

Would you ever dream of eating a popsicle with the wrapper still on? Get into the music and taste it.

⑲ Are You a Piano Student?

Voltaire said...

"It is more important to be interesting than it is to be exact."

Most of us have a lot of interesting students.

I remember a teacher asking me how many students I taught and I said "two." Taken aback, she said "Is that all?"

"I have twenty who play the piano, but only two who are true students of the instrument."

No Limits 20

Everyone is gifted in one area.

There is no limit to human potential
in the pursuit of procrastination.

The Good Doctor 21

Piano students should listen to the good doctor for his
view on accountability.

"You have brains in your head.
You have feet in your shoes.
You can steer yourself
any direction you choose."

Oh, the Places You'll Go!
*~ **Dr. Seuss***

㉒ It's Easy When You Know It

You know this piece, but can you play it? It looks so complicated because of all the accidentals. Your job is to simplify to make it easier to read. Give up?

"Happy Birthday," minus abundant accidentals if read in the usual key of F

Why, Oh Why, Can't I?  ㉓

The bee should not be able to fly. Its wings are the wrong shape, its body too fat, its proportion unscientific. But the bee doesn't know all this, so he just flies anyway.

We can become too analytical, try too hard, strain too much. The body is incredibly designed, orchestrated, integrated. It works for us.

Metronome Mystery ㉔

"H-m-m-m-m, why aren't your fingerprints on the metronome this week?"

That's what I ask a student whose counting is erratic.

Unfair Advantage ㉕

When teachers return from the highly charged atmosphere of a convention, clinic, or workshop, remember that your students didn't attend.

You're way up high, just dying to try new ideas, and they're innocently walking into a piano lesson.

26 It's Not What You Think

The goal is to play difficult music with ease.
Too many of us play difficult music with difficulty.

27 Never Louder
Than Lovely

WARNING

When you observe a f or ff in the score, avoid harshness through imagery such as velvet covered keys. Use arm weight to cushion the sound, remembering that volume and beauty can coexist if you are never louder than lovely.

Guilty As Charged

NEVER REPEAT WHAT YOU CANNOT DO!

㉙ The More You Know

A little harmonic awareness and rhythmic discipline never hurt anyone.

㉚ Play From The Heart

If your goal is to communicate, your playing is more likely to be

♫ *Unforgettable* ♫

not regrettable.

㉛ Wrist Watch

The bracelet of small bones at the base of the hand is commonly known as the wrist. Lift it gently or energetically (as dictated by the music) to begin and end a phrase. In order to approach the keyboard, the wrist is usually called to serve.

Good Advice

In baseball, when you come up to bat,
swing hard... just in case you hit the ball.

This is good advice
for all musicians.
Remember the
Hokey Pokey ending:
"Put your whole self in."

Review the Basics

Professional baseball players report for batting
practice (BP) before every game. They practice the
basic skills of pitching, catching, hitting, and running,
so when the game is on the line, they can perform.
This baseball skillset can be summarized into the basic
gestures at the piano: drop, lift, throw, and rotate.

㉞ Obedience School

The first two commands a puppy learns:

Sit

Stay

work equally
well for
aspiring
pianists.

㉟ Wrinkle Wreck

The earlier you iron out the
wrinkles in a new piece,
the smoother it will flow.

What You Need Now

Choose your most troublesome measures
to lavish with attention. This will bring them
to the level of your best measures.

A good example is:
The most unlovable child in the family
needs the most love.

Primed to Practice

Sing these two verses to the tune of Frère Jacques:

Are you grateful,
are you grateful
For your gift
And your time?
Give up your excuses,
Rearrange your choices,
Now's the prime
Of your life.

Why make music,
why make music?
It's so hard,
What's the use?
It's because of Mozart,
Beethoven and Chopin,
They inspire,
Light your fire

㊳ Versatile Sixteenth Notes

Don't hit the panic button when you see sixteenth notes. In the Beethoven example below, they carry the rhythmic momentum.

Sixteenth notes are not always virtuosic. They can be lyrical.

Sonata Op.13, Mvt. 2 (Pathetique)
meas. 1-4

㊴ Priorities, Please

EGGS DO NOT FLY!

They hatch first. Never underestimate the value of incubation. So many students lack the patience to spend any time in this phase. They want to go straight to flying!

Mezzo Blah

No one should ever feel moderato
about music.

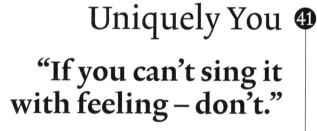

Make sure you and
your students don't
reach **burnout**
at the same time.

Uniquely You ④①

"If you can't sing it with feeling – don't."

~ Patsy Cline
Country Singer

㊷ Finger Fact

The fingers are foolish, but smart enough to learn after a few repetitions. Use mind control for those wayward fingers.

㊸ X-Rated

How would you rate your practice time? Have you checked all the X's?

- X–plore

- X–amine

- X–periment

- X–aggerate

X–cel

Lowering The Bar 44

Because our students are so over-scheduled and under-rehearsed, we have reached a higher level of mediocrity than in the past.

Mindful Repetition 45

"Knowledge is not skill. Knowledge plus 10,000 times is skill."

~ Shinichi Suzuki

Be Careful 46

A vase can survive a chip or a few cracks, but if it falls into too many pieces, it cannot be restored. Think about this image when you are practicing a piece with too many glitches.

④ A Work in Progress

Practice doesn't make perfect, but it does make permanent. Practice is about increasing your repertoire of ways to recover from your mistakes.

④ Seeking a Better Balance

Teachers should beware of excessive emphasis on performance quality in their student's repertoire. It speeds up polishing but slows down learning.

④ A Game Changer

When my husband retired it was like having a grand piano in the kitchen...

Very nice,

but still in the way.

U & Music, ㊿
Always Inseparable

Remember to put the

U

in m**U**sic

Whenever **U** practice

and perform.

Q & A
with a Former Student,
Current Physician

Q: What are some significant components of Suzanne's teaching that you remember – her language, her approach to technique, her practice requirements, her attitude toward competitions and performance preparation?

A: **She was strict but warm and inspiring at the same time. Competitions were important but were only meant to motivate and improve to a higher level. Performances were to be taken seriously and there was never substitute for hard work.**

Q: What was your first impression of her group lessons and how did it change with time?

A: **I was intimidated at first, partly because I was the only boy in the advanced class. The high level of her studio pushed me to want to be better.**

Q: How has Suzanne helped to further your own musicianship and career?

A: **She taught me how to teach myself. It was a wonderful mentorship and friendship. She taught me about music and life.**

~ Dr. Christopher Shih, Gastroenterologist
First Place, Van Cliburn Amateur Competition

Wisdom

❶ Have To, Love To

A good plan is to begin your practice session with something you need and end with something you love. Remember, practicing expires in 24 hours. It must be created every day.

If it's too difficult to keep track of the days you should practice, there is an easy solution:

Practice on the days you eat.

~ Paraphrased from a Suzuki Parent Guide

❷ Two Wrongs Don't Make It Right

What is the difference between right and wrong?

Don't practice until you play it right (wrong)
Practice until you can't play it wrong (right)!

Bach *Minuet In G* (Anna Magdalena Notebook)

Music En Route to Magic ❸

If your practice time is low on magic moments,
try this – it's as easy as 1. 2. 3.

1. Widen your dynamic range

2. Master the 2-note slur

3. AC-CEN-TU-ATE AR-TI-CU-LA-TION

4 It All Begins With Fingering

"More is lost through poor fingering than can ever be regained through all conceivable artistry and good taste."

~ C. P. E. Bach

Fingering first or problems last.

How many of us admit to *fumbling carelessly* when we could be *fingering carefully*?

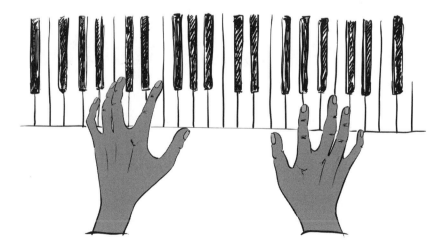

You Are What and How You Practice ❺

We acquire good and bad habits the same way...
through repetition.

The next step is to ask yourself, "What is my goal
as I repeat these measures?"

Rhymes to Remember ❻

Find Beauty in Duty

There's a lot of S-L-O-W in GROW

❼ What is Your E-Q?

How can you improve your expression quotient?

Your music sounds like Pinocchio, a beautifully crafted puppet, but there's no heart.

You are very observant of all the markings in this Nocturne, but I am more interested in what is not on the page.

Instead of thinking about the notes on the page, focus on the secrets the composer wants to share.

S-H-H-SSH

The piano speaks
so eloquently,
you don't have to say a

W _ _ _.

Attitude Adjustment ❾

If you practice because you have to, it seems like a
burden. Practice because you are able to,
and regard it as a gift.

To Know and Not To Do ❿
is Not To Know

It isn't that we don't know what to do, it is that we
don't do what we know.

Examples of what you know and fail to do:

Practice slowly

Have several starting places in every piece

Breathe – watch and listen to singers

*Anatomy of a phrase – the first note is soft, the last note is
softer. Everything else is louder.*

⑪ Mt. Everest Beckons

It is important to remember that composers write music for the piano, not the pianist. However, even the most difficult works are meant to be played by someone.

Liszt ~ Mephisto Waltz No. 1

⑫ Focus

It is possible to do more than one thing at a time.

It is not possible to think of more than one thought at a time.

Can you find the distraction?

Would you be able to maintain your focus? Your mind must be focused on the music, not all the distractions in your life.

When NOT to Practice ⓭

H-A-L-T your practice if you are:

Hungry · **A**ngry · **L**onely · **T**ired

One-Trick Pony ⓮

The piano can do only one trick...

It can get softer.

Take advantage of this feature and always listen
THROUGH all the long notes.

Match

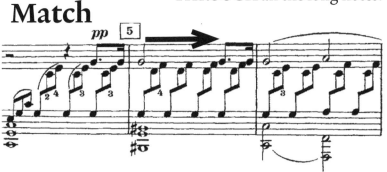

Beethoven *Moonlight Sonata Op. 27 No. 2 (m. 4 – 6)*

The beginning of the next note must match
the end of the last sound.

⓯ Final, Futile, Fatal

**"Success is not final;
failure is not fatal."**

~ Winston Churchill

"Mistakes are not futile."

~ Suzanne Guy

⓰ Days of Our Lives

**"The two most important
days in your life are the day
you are born and the day
you figure out why."**

~ Mark Twain

From the Stage 🄱

Remember, you are an actor who just happens to play the piano and whose stage is the keyboard.

Project and Communicate

Hand in Hand 🄲

Most people with low self esteem have high self-pity.

Every Minute Counts 🄳

Learn the value of one minute rather than the waste of one hour.

Did you know, with the metronome set to quarter note = 80, you can play 5 1/3 scales four octaves in sixteenth-note rhythm (4 notes per tick) in one minute?

⑳ Confidence, Not Arrogance

Let your genes speak.

If you've done your homework,
let go and let it flow.

Play from trust, not fear.

In other words,
do not get in your own way.

㉑ Make Haste at First

Be sure to practice on lesson day!

Students typically consider the lesson their practice
session, forgetting that 80% of new information will
be lost by the next day. By the third day, it's as if all the
new information is erased.

Oh Dear, Where is the Melody? ㉒

The time to bring out a melody is while you're young – the better to give yourself pleasure all your musical life.

Treat every phrase as if you lived another day just to play it.

Discipline Trumps Desire ㉓

Advice from Mark Twain:

"Every day do something you do not want to do."

Discipline is daily.

Motivation is fragile. It is also fickle and temporary. Practicing is an acquired taste. Begin the acquisition.

㉔ Sing Out Strong

When singers sing, it is not the words themselves, but the meaning behind them that people listen to. The words must first be passed through the heart on the way to the mouth.

When pianists play, it is the sound that serves as the magnet calling the audience to listen. Note-by-note playing falls on deaf ears.

㉕ Pretend to Conduct

The path to tonal beauty is more than a little move here and a quick jump there.

It is a symphony of gestures.

Watch the first violinist in the orchestra. Notice how physically involved their performance is. The rest of the string players get their cue from all that energy.

You Can't Start at the End ㉖

Everyone comes to the piano from the same point. You fell in love with the sound because you heard someone play a piece beautifully. But you did not hear someone practice. You cannot begin at the finish line. When you hear a truly compelling performance, just know it is not an accident.

Wrong and Strong ㉗

If you must play a wrong note, play it strong. If you combine wrong and weak, you have made two mistakes.

And while you're at it, play dissonance with confidence. Otherwise, people think you've misplayed the chord.

㉘ From The Inside Out

CHIP, CHIP AWAY!

That huge chunk of marble
called practice is waiting to
turn into something beautiful.
For Michelangelo, it turned
into David.

㉙ Delve Deeper

Teachers see possibilities.
Students see limitations.

What really sets one student apart from another
is the unique imagination they each bring
to interpretation.

This puzzle is an exercise
in creativity that makes
a lasting impression.
Here are the instructions:
Connect all 9 dots with four
continuous straight lines.
It is immediately apparent that 8 dots can be
connected on the perimeter but what about the dot
in the middle? The answer is on WISDOM #50.

Mt. Everest ③⓪
Calls Again (See #11)

If you see a man on top of a mountain, notice he did not fall there.

He climbed step by step.

Hot and Cold ③①

Often we go for the FIRE in a piece, but we forget that ICE can be equally appropriate. Rachmaninoff's *G# Minor Prelude* is a notable example.

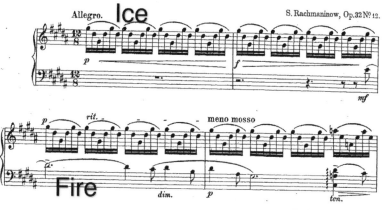

G# Minor Prelude Op. 32 No. 12

I think of birch trees wearing icicles that shiver in the dead of winter.

㉜ Seek and You Will Find

When you see the *p*, think "project" instead of sounding puny. Did you know that Beethoven's favorite dynamic marking is *p*? Twenty of his 32 piano sonatas begin *piano,* and four of the most famous open with *pp*.

Sometimes the most special spot in a piece is the softest. Look over your books of music and draw a light circle around the *p* and *pp* markings. One of my first teachers called it "shading." If you can widen your dynamic range, it's like playing in living color.

㉝ Not Effective Immediately

p + mp − mp + mf − mf mf + ff − ff and *ff − ff + mf mf − mf + mp − mp + p*

...are not dynamic signs. They are instructions for gradual increase or decrease of intensity.

If a
refers to eight notes, there must be eight degrees of loudness starting softly. Measure your crescendo and diminuendo in small increments, as the illustration indicates.

The Four Agreements 34

For many sports teams, coaches require their players to read and heed the principles in an easy-to-read book by Don Miguel Ruiz. *The Four Agreements* has simplified some of the most important core values we share, as Ruiz challenges us to abide by them. For musicians, one of those agreements has particular impact: never allow your judges to turn you into a victim.

If you are able to silence the negative voices that cripple your confidence, count yourself victorious.

P-I-A-N-O Spells Relief 35

Busy people answer to so many calls, demands and crises, that it is a welcome safe haven to settle into the music of the day.

Somewhere between lethargy and hysteria is a steady, productive pace toward eventual mastery.

㊱ Robots: KEEP OUT

Speech is full of in**FLEC**tion.

MUsic is a LANGuage of
in**FLEC**tion in Sound.

Inflection is more subtle than dynamics.

㊲ A Delicate Dilemma

Most students view music lessons as another activity
to add to an already jammed schedule. Instead, ask
yourselves this question:

**What are you willing to give up to achieve
your goals and to ensure steady progress?**

Start with releasing your excuses.

In a Word 38

Here is a one-word summary of the four
style periods of music:

Baroque – Dependable

Classical – Dramatic

Romantic – Dynamic

ConTEMPORARY - Diverse

Smooth As Silk 39

Legato is a lifelong quest.

The greatest artists are always working to perfect
their legato, an illusion for all pianists. Here are two
experiments to try:

**Pour water from a pitcher slowly and evenly
in a steady stream to simulate legato.**

**As you exit a room, sneak away by masking
footfalls noiselessly.**

Now you know the feeling of legato.

⑩ Popularity Contest

Practicing does not deserve its bad reputation. Most people like pizza and Harry Potter.

Why is practicing not popular?

Set small reachable goals in short sessions and know that joy waits for you. It's all about attitude and accomplishment. If one's attitude is set to hate practicing, one finds excuses to delay and avoid it altogether.

㉛ It's So Hard

The art of listening cannot be taught by talking.

Teachers: If you want your students to listen, demonstrate as much as possible and talk as little as possible. Take your cue from stage actors who elevate dialogue to a level far beyond plain talk.

Actors use a lot of dialogue, but they never just talk. In order to get the audience to hang on every word, they use dramatic pause, gesture, and emotion to get their points across.

Lessons From a Child Movie Star 42

Mrs. Temple used to rehearse her four-year old daughter's lines in upcoming scenes at dinner time. Just before the first take, her parting words were:

"Sparkle, Shirley, Sparkle."

Insert your own name in place of Shirley's, and remember that feeling whenever you perform at the piano.

Pablo Casal's Secret 43

Pablo Casals was as much a philosopher as he was a celebrated cellist. An adoring fan asked Casals (when he was 84 years old) why he continued to practice four hours a day.

"I keep practicing because I believe I am making progress."

④ Too Much The Same

There is no exact repetition in music. Be sure to contrast the treatment of the same musical information. Think of all those consecutive Eflats in the right hand melody of Chopin's Aeolian Harp Etude, Op. 25, No. 1. Underneath is a measure of ⟨⟨ followed by a measure of ⟩⟩. Unfortunately, if there is no inflection, it sounds like your piano is being tuned.

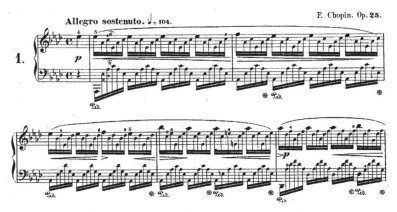

Chopin's *Aeolian Harp Etude Op. 25, No. 1*

Starving Artists 45

If you think of the vast quantity of literature written for the piano, it is a feast for those who sight read well. Alas, far too many pianists are starving at this banquet.

The natural ability to sight play without training occurs about as often as the child of three who teaches himself to read. Obviously, very few are so blessed. Yet the percentage of children who learn to read books is infinitely higher than the number of students who learn to read music.

The key is early saturation and reinforcement of music that matches your reading level.

Technically Speaking 46

You can do anything if you have the technique because it allows your imagination to speak. Otherwise, you have a wee small voice at the keyboard.

The root of the word technique is Greek, and surprisingly, it means art. Thus when one practices technique, expressive, imaginative playing is virtually guaranteed.

47 In My Bones

Did you know that 54 of the 206 bones in the body are in your hands?

Use them wisely.

48 Elephant vs. Flea

Use the elephant/flea approach to memorizing a piece. By delaying the process of memory, it becomes as huge as an elephant to tackle. When you do a little bit each day, it's more like a flea. Inch by inch, it's a cinch. Yard by yard, it's too hard.

49 Easy as 1-2-3

When it's time to perform, you must bring three things with you:

1. What you know about the piece

2. What you know about the composer

3. What you know about the piano

Time to show, tell and share.

Start Here:

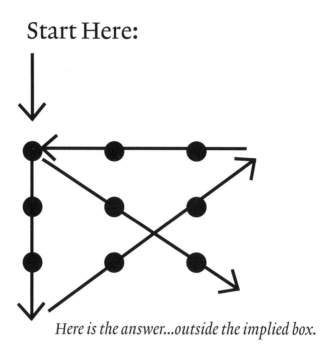

Here is the answer...outside the implied box.

There are several possibilities as long as the solution forces thinking outside the implied box. What a perfect illustration for musicians to follow suit. A representative example is the "The Wild Rider" by Robert Schumann. The piece begins and ends in A minor but the middle section should have been in C Major. Instead, the composer treats us to F major, breaking with the tradition of modulating to the relative Major.

An advance sample of Suzanne's Master Lessons
to be collected in a future book:

Chopin's Prelude
in E minor, op. 28, no. 4

Chopin loved this prelude above all others, choosing it along with Mozart's *Requiem* to be played at his funeral. The secret of mastering the impact of its achingly beautiful melody is in highlighting its chromaticism. The slow descent from C to G#, a minor third, takes eight full measures. Create your sound for the melody by imagining a sad moment in life, such as the death of a family pet or the loss of a special friend who moved away. Play the right hand with the pad of each finger, caressing the key from an almost flat hand position. Note the right hand carries the single-line melody throughout, but it must sing out above first inversion chords in the left hand. Think of the two hands as if they speak two languages because the technique is completely different. The left hand chords are best played with the keys half down; in other words, take care to depress each chord before the keys come all the way back.

One must listen carefully to each harmonic change, allowing the finger that plays the change of harmony to emerge from the overall soft dynamic level. I believe that all masterworks, no matter the length, have a special spot or magic moment. As short as this prelude is, I had great difficulty narrowing down to one. The obvious choice is the climax in measure 17 where the highest pitch and the only forte converge. However, the d natural in measure 12 is especially tragic. This measure is the only one with a triplet and the absence of that relentless eighth note drone. A perfect authentic cadence closes the prelude after a deafening silence.

PHOTO: William McIntosh

How Suzanne West Guy
Came To Teach Piano

Her first love was the piano.

"This is your lucky day," my mother said.

"The piano is going to be delivered this afternoon!"

That "lucky day" phrase stayed with Suzanne West 12 years later when she greeted her first piano student. By today's standards, Suzanne would be called a late beginner, starting lessons at the age of ten after begging since the first grade. Her teacher was Mr. Johnson and John Thompson's *Teaching Little Fingers to Play* became her constant companion. She could hardly turn the pages fast enough. In December, she played "Swans on the Lake," her first recital piece in the tall book. She finished all five books in the series in two years, and soon after, transferred to Mary Kirk, the mother of her best friend, Sarah. They often had sleepovers, and at Sarah's house, they would read through Mrs.

Suzanne (right) and her friend Sarah seated at the piano.

Kirk's music library – especially duets – as many as they could find. When they finished with duets, they divided solos between the hands.

Mrs. Kirk presented her students in annual recitals with supportive parents in the audience. "My father," explained Suzanne, "asked if he could arrive later, just in time for my portion on the program. My mother was the classical music lover." Suzanne remembers her father's comment after she played a rousing version of Chopin's Military Polonaise. "Do you realize how many times you could have ended that piece?"

In 1955 Suzanne saw a movie that was to impact her future in ways she could not have envisioned. It was *A Man Called Peter*, based on a book by the same name. The story was told by Peter Marshall, who rose to the level of national chaplain of the U.S. Senate. His wife Catherine was played by Jean Peters. The background in many scenes was the gothic campus of Agnes Scott College where Catherine was a senior. Suzanne decided before high school that the liberal arts college for women outside Atlanta would be her home for four years in the early sixties.

Armed with a BA degree in piano performance and a Spanish minor, Suzanne's first job was teaching Spanish at Brookville High School near Lynchburg, VA. She and a Latin teacher were the entire foreign language department. The collegebound students elected Latin whereas the jocks chose Spanish, previously taught by the football coach. Suzanne had been an exchange student in Bogotà, Columbia the summer after graduation, so she was excited to experiment with language immersion in her classes, even the Spanish 1 section. Her first teaching experience was a colossal failure because her students had signed up for an easy B while Miss West had visions of turning out bilingual graduates.

Although Suzanne was not invited to return after her first year, she did receive a much better offer – a marriage proposal from civil engineer Louis L. Guy. He was surprised to learn that his new wife started a campaign for a piano in their first apartment. He thought she would find a job teaching Spanish in a different location.

The next four years flew by with the arrival of three sons and a grand piano (a Chickering 6-footer). Without fanfare or drumroll, Suzanne began her career as a neighborhood piano teacher in five locations, all in Virginia with the exception of three years in Salisbury, MD. She always started with a small class of beginners and considered herself fortunate to learn as she taught. She used an assortment of methods, stressing lateral reinforcement and saturation in material for students to read.

When the family of five moved to Annandale, Suzanne was determined to plan for a more permanent stay where she could teach beyond the elementary level. Lessons would be expanded to an hour and she would introduce her students to four-hand and two-piano literature. She longed to explore the concerto library and knew the first step was to purchase a second piano. A Steinway M was moved from a tiny town in southwest Virginia, a neglected instrument Louis found in the corner of a client's garage.

Those 23 years in Northern Virginia produced scores of successful students who enjoy performing as well as building careers in pedagogy and professional development. It is especially gratifying to encounter many of these former students at national keyboard conferences, as officers in their local associations and presenters of master classes and lectures. Most of Suzanne's students, of course, went into other fields, but they never let go of music's hold on them. In fact, they are turning up in amateur competitions in the U.S. and abroad.

She credits regular lessons with teachers Nelita True and Grace McFarlane, who informed and inspired her teaching. While in Northern Virginia, she taught pedagogy classes at George Mason University and Peabody Conservatory. Her lectures and workshops began by accident. She was program chair for the Springfield Music Club and the scheduled guest artist was renowned Hungarian pianist Ylda Novik, who called the day of the meeting to cancel due to illness. When Suzanne informed the president to alert the members, she said, "It's too late to contact anyone else, so you give the program." Suzanne presented her first impromptu lecture on the Bach Inventions that day.

For the next 27 years Suzanne gave lectures and master classes on 20 different topics in 42 states. Her most popular lecture was "How to Practice as Little as Possible." Music teachers have soaked up her knowledge like a sponge at MTNA conferences and affiliate state and local chapters. She has judged competitions in Hong Kong, published children's books about music, edited Expressive Etudes (a deliberate title to join expression and technique), and written numerous articles in various music journals.

Where does a teacher go after decades in a premier area like Washington D.C.? A second chapter began in 1993, that lasted another 17 years and brought the grand total to 45 years and well over 1,000 students. Suzanne thought she would mark 50 years as an independent piano teacher, matching the 50:50 examples in *Wit and Wisdom*. Yet she wouldn't have been able to collaborate on this project without the unexpected windfall of time.

One day, of no particular significance, Suzanne noticed a twinge in her left fifth finger. The one that played the low notes in a Chopin nocturne. That was the first visible sign of Parkinson's Disease. This disease of the nervous system that impacts movement, had been developing silently for decades. There have been highs, lows and plateaus during the fourteen years that Suzanne has been living and teaching with Parkinson's Disease.

In spite of the limitations imposed by Parkinson's, Suzanne continues to teach piano lessons to a small class of adult students, many whom are piano teachers themselves. They understandingly allow her the flexibility to visit her children and grandchildren.

Music plays on. Each new day brings more challenges and limitations, but she is grateful that her witty wisdom is still intact.

Teaching Teachers How to Teach

Lecturing at Wheaton College and Conservatory

Teaching in Graz Austria

PHOTO: Joanna Lea Garber

Dr. Tonya M. Holland

is a graduate of James Madison University with a DMA in Piano Performance, Literature and Pedagogy. She is a nationally certified teacher through the Music Teachers National Association (MTNA) and a past president of the Tidewater Music Teachers Forum. Dr. Holland served as State Theory Chair for the Virginia Music Teachers Association, working with a team of VMTA teachers to include twentieth-century idioms into pre-college private lesson curricula. Her theory research has been published under the title "20th-Century Theory, It's About Time: The Compositional Techniques of Maurice Ravel" in the *American Music Teacher* magazine.

Dr. Holland has owned her own music studio since 1993, teaching a wide variety of ages and levels in piano, music theory, and voice in private and group instruction. She held church positions as organist, pianist and music coordinator from 1990 through 2015. She is currently pianist for JMU Chorale and the newly established Mozart and More Trio, accompanies vocal and instrumental soloists in Virginia, and assists with music for Harrisonburg Baptist Church.

In addition to being a collaborative artist, she is adjunct professor at James Madison University, Bridgewater College, and previously Mary Baldwin College. Her courses include Piano Pedagogy, Private Piano Lessons, Music Theory, and Intro to Western Music. Other projects include founding administrator and teacher in community outreach adult group piano classes through JMU Music Academy, Administrator of the JMU Vocal Arts Camp, and conducting the Page County Community Choir in Luray, VA.

The two pianists hanging out at Starbucks!

Photo: Abbie Rae Menard

Let it Grow! Let it Grow! Let it Grow!

A letter from Suzanne Guy to her students

Dear Students,

The is your lucky day! The day you start your 21-day practice progress in the absence of lessons. In case you need a visual reminder of what this project looks like, compare the two photographs – before and after. Look carefully at the before photo – the Lady Banks roses climbing the brick wall at the studio entrance (where it's all green leaves). This was last year's photo, but can you believe the difference? It's now an explosion of white flowers. Such dramatic growth is entirely possible in plants and people! While you cannot see them grow overnight, it does happen over time. So I'll be expecting to see you in full bloom after the break!

Love,
Mrs. Guy

Before   After